Let's Visit the Farm

written by Elizabeth Bennett

Silver Dolphin

San Diego, California

Welcome to Sunny Acres Farm. My name is Sam and I'm a farmer.

Like most farms, Sunny Acres Farm is a family farm. I grew up here, and now I live and work here with my family!

Running a farm takes a lot of work. There are fields to be plowed, crops to be planted, cows to be milked, and many other jobs. Everyone in my family helps out—even my kids.

Have you ever been to a farm? I would be happy to show you around and introduce you to my family. You can even meet some of the animals that live at Sunny Acres Farm.

Come on in—the gate is open!

Farm Work

Farms are where fruits, vegetables, and grains are grown, and farm animals are raised. Some farms are big and others are really small.

At Sunny Acres Farm we raise cows, pigs, and sheep. We also grow most of the food that our animals eat, as well as vegetables to sell at the market. All season long we plow, plant, or **harvest**. There is so much work to do that my family can't do it alone. I hire farmworkers to help us.

A worker helps by plowing a field to get it ready for planting.

bale

At the end of the summer, the workers gather hay into bales.

My wife, Jenna, is in charge of getting the vegetable garden ready for planting seeds in the spring.

At harvesttime, everyone helps out! My daughter, Kim, especially likes to pick pumpkins.

Farm Tools

We need lots of machines and tools. The tractor is probably the most important machine on a farm. Sometimes it is even called the farmer's best friend! My tractor makes my work much easier because it can pull and lift heavy things. With special attachments, a tractor can help me clear a field or plant seeds. It is also helpful for harvesting **crops** and baling hay.

The farmer's best friend!

The tractor's big back wheels allow it to drive through hard earth and wet mud. The smaller front wheels help the tractor turn.

baler

plow

While machines do the big jobs, we also use many of the same tools gardeners use. We use shovels to dig holes and clean out stalls. A pitchfork comes in handy for picking up and spreading hay and leaves.

shovel

pitchfork

wheelbarrow

The Barn

When you think of a farm, you probably picture a big red barn. And you are right! Just about every farm has a barn, and many are red because red paint was inexpensive and easy to make or find in the old days. The barn is used to store farm equipment and to protect animals from bad weather. Barns have really big doors so it is easy to get equipment and animals in and out.

Barns usually have a silo. A silo is a tall, round structure that is used to store feed for animals or grain that the farmer will sell. The round shape makes the silo strong. It is also very tall so it can hold a lot of grain.

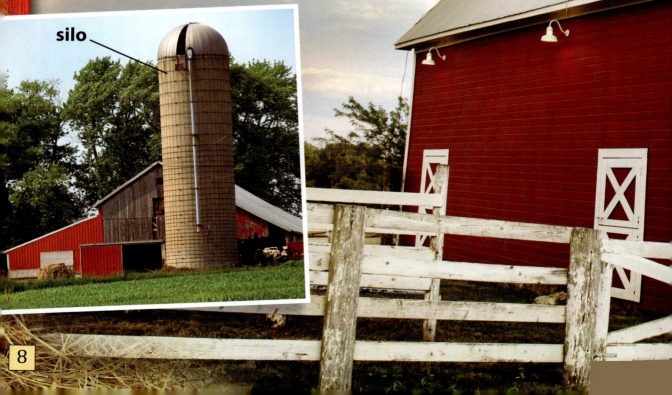

silo

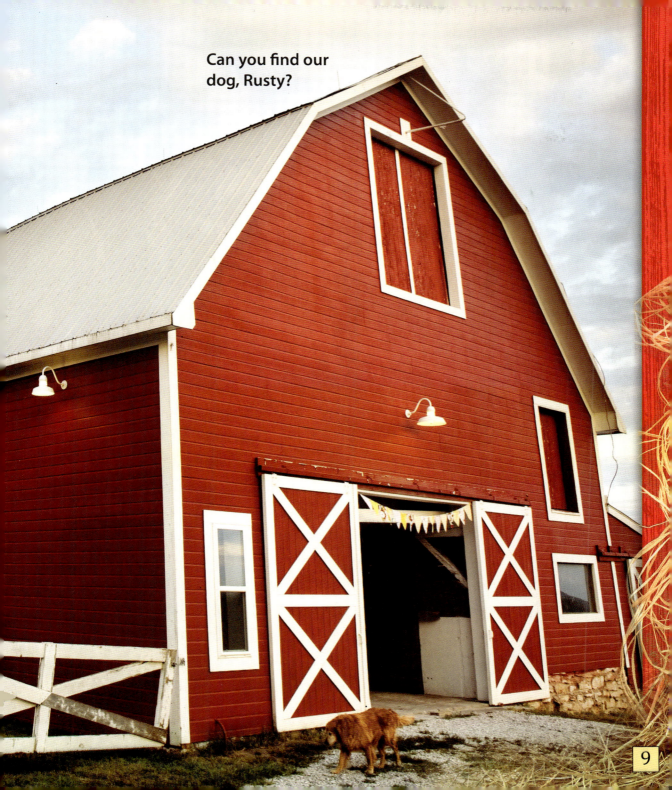

Can you find our dog, Rusty?

Dairy Farming

Sunny Acres Farm has lots of cows, and our most important job is to make sure they are happy and healthy!

Don't become a farmer if you aren't good at getting up early in the morning. Cows need to be milked two times a day. At my farm, we first milk them at four o'clock in the morning! Then the cows are milked again at four o'clock in the afternoon.

In the old days, farmers milked cows by hand, but today we use machines. We bring our cows into the milking barn and give them a bucket of food to eat. Then we attach hoses to the cows' **udders**, and a pump gently sucks out the milk.

Milk trucks come every day to pick up the fresh milk and take it to a factory, where it is put into bottles and cartons. From there, it goes to the stores where people can buy it.

Dairy cows like these are called Holsteins.

The milking machine has hoses that attach to the udders. Each cow has four udders.

Cows

For the first six weeks of its life, a calf drinks milk from its mother and doesn't eat any other food. By the time the calf is three months old, it is ready to spend the day in the field, eating grass with the other cows. Cows are very friendly animals and enjoy living in big **herds**.

A cow will keep producing milk even after the calf is all grown up, as long as the cow is milked every day.

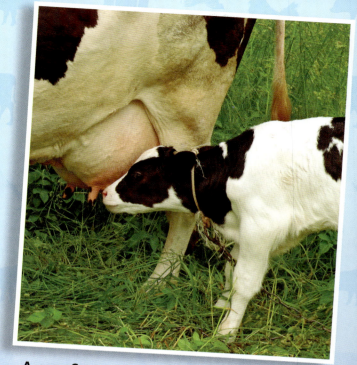

A cow first produces milk when she has a calf.

Moo!

A dairy cow can produce over 20,000 pounds of milk each year!

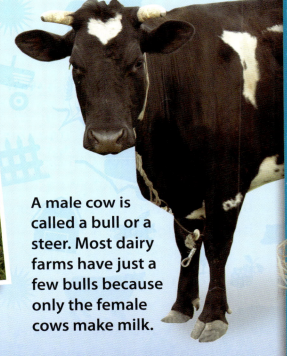

A male cow is called a bull or a steer. Most dairy farms have just a few bulls because only the female cows make milk.

Sheep

We also have some sheep on Sunny Acres Farm. Sheep have thick wool, or **fleece**, on their bodies. The fleece can be used to make things like sweaters, blankets, mittens, and other items of clothing.

   We use a special tool to cut the wool off our sheep. Cutting the wool is called shearing—and just like when you get a haircut, shearing doesn't hurt the sheep at all!

Most sheep are sheared once a year.

BAA!

Some of our animals have ear tags.
The tag helps us keep track of each animal.

Female sheep, or **ewes**, usually have their babies in the spring. Most ewes have one or two babies each year. Baby sheep are called lambs. When a lamb is born, it is about the size of a small dog, and is very shaky when it tries to stand up. By the time it is two months old, the lamb will be romping and playing in the field.

Horses

In the old days, horses did a lot of work on a farm. Now most of their work is done by machines. But we still have a few horses here at Sunny Acres. Riding them is a great way to travel around the farm, and it sure is a lot of fun!

These horses are pulling an old-fashioned plow.

Neigh!

Here are Chestnut and Blaze with Jasper, their foal!

We have a **mare** named Chestnut and a **stallion** named Blaze. Last summer, Chestnut had a **foal**. My son, Evan, named him Jasper. When Jasper was only a few hours old, he was already standing up and walking! Jasper is growing really quickly. He will be almost fully grown by the time he is two years old.

Horses eat mostly hay and grass, so they spend a lot of time grazing in the meadow. In the evening, we bring the horses into the barn so they can sleep. Horses are able to sleep standing up!

Look at him run—he sure is beautiful!

Pigs

Not many animals are cuter than a baby pig! Our pig had nine piglets this spring, and they sure are busy!

Pigs have flat noses called **snouts**, small eyes, and curly tails. Their ears are large and floppy. They come in many colors, shapes, and sizes. Pigs have short, stiff hairs on their bodies called bristles.

Can you find all nine piglets?

Oink!

You may be surprised to know that pigs are usually very clean animals. However, when the weather is hot, they love to roll in mud. The mud keeps them cool and protects them from the sun.

Our pigs spend most of their time eating. We give them food every day, but they also like to hunt for food, using their snouts to sniff around in the dirt for things to nibble on.

What has this pig found?

Chickens

Every morning, Jenna and the kids go to our chicken coop to collect eggs. Most of our chickens lay one egg a day. We use some of the eggs ourselves, and sell the rest to a local market.

We raise our chickens from chicks. Chicks have fluffy yellow feathers called **down**. As they get older, the chicks begin to look more like grown-up chickens. Their feathers will change color to brown, white, or gray. They will grow red crowns and waddles.

crown

waddle

Cluck!

Roosters are fancy!

Our chickens love to scratch at the ground. They are looking for insects and grubs to eat!

down

Chickens like to be together with other chickens in groups called **flocks**. Male chickens, or roosters, often fight with each other, so we have only one. Our rooster helps us wake up in the morning in time to milk the cows. *Cock-a-doodle-doo!*

Bees

What is that buzzing sound? It's our bees, of course! Let's go take a look—but don't get too close!

On a farm, bees live in a box-shaped wooden hive. There are thousands of bees living inside this one. The bees gather sweet juice from flowers called **nectar** and bring it back to the hive. Inside the hive, bees are busy building a honeycomb and making honey from the nectar.

I put on special clothes to collect the honeycombs from the hive. I don't want to get stung by the bees. This honeycomb is dripping with delicious honey. Yum!

Do you like goats? We don't have any at Sunny Acres, but our neighbors down the road do. Let's go pay them a visit!

We eat some of the honey, but most of it goes to the market!

Goats

These goats are raised for their milk, just like our cows. The milk is used to make cheese, which our friends sell to markets. They also make soap from the goats' milk.

Most goats have horns. Their hair is straighter and thinner than a sheep's wool.

Goat cheese!

Maaa!

Goats, like cows and sheep, are herd animals.

If you look closely at a goat's eyes, you will see that the dark part of each eye is rectangular in shape. This helps the goat see a big area without turning its head!

Many people think that goats will eat anything, but they don't actually eat things like cans and cardboard. They will, however, sniff or chew things to find out if they are good to eat. Goats eat grass, shrubs, weeds, hay, and leaves from trees.

Let's head back to my farm. I want to show you what we are growing!

Some goats have beards!

Fruits and Vegetables

We grow grains on our farm for the animals, but we also have fields that are planted with vegetables. We grow broccoli, carrots, and lettuce, as well as fruits like strawberries and melons.

Different vegetables are ready to be picked at different times of the year. Sweet peas and lettuce can be harvested in the late spring. We have a berry patch with juicy blueberries and strawberries. They are picked in the early summer months.

snap peas

strawberries

lettuce

Throughout the summer we harvest most of our **produce**. The tomatoes are red and ripe and ready to pick in the late summer.

In the fall, our pumpkins are big and orange and perfect for Halloween jack-o'-lanterns. We have a small **orchard** with apple and pear trees. Their fruit is ready to be picked in the fall.

tomatoes

apple tree

The Market

Every week during the harvest season we load up our truck and head to the local farmers' market. It's a great way to sell extra produce. It's also a great place to meet other farmers. We can see what grew well this year and share stories.

We set up a table and display our fruits and vegetables in baskets. The market is very crowded and busy. Kim and Evan love to help the customers.

Have you ever been to a farmers' market? Markets are filled with all kinds of colors and smells. You can check out all the stands and buy fresh fruits and vegetables. You can also find foods like honey, apple cider, eggs, and homemade breads and pies. You will probably get to taste some treats that come fresh from a farm. Yum!

I hope you enjoyed visiting Sunny Acres Farm. Come visit again soon!

Glossary

crop: A plant that is grown in large amounts and often sold as food.

down: The soft feathers of a bird.

ewe: A female sheep.

fleece: A sheep's woolly coat.

flock: A group of animals, usually birds, of one kind that lives and travels together.

foal: A young horse.

harvest: Picking all of the crops in a field or a garden.

herd: A large group of animals.

mare: A female horse.

nectar: A sweet liquid that bees collect from flowers and turn into honey.

orchard: A field or farm where fruit trees are grown.

produce: Things that are grown for eating, especially fruits and vegetables.

snout: The long, front part of an animal's head.

stallion: An adult male horse.

udder: The baglike part of a cow that hangs down and contains glands that make milk.

Let's Build a Farm!

Instructions
&
Press-outs

You've learned all about what it takes to run a farm. Now, build one yourself! There are many ways to arrange your farm. Use these instructions as a guide and then create your own unique layout. Start by laying the case and tray flat as shown. These will be the "ground" for your farm.

Use either side of the tray.

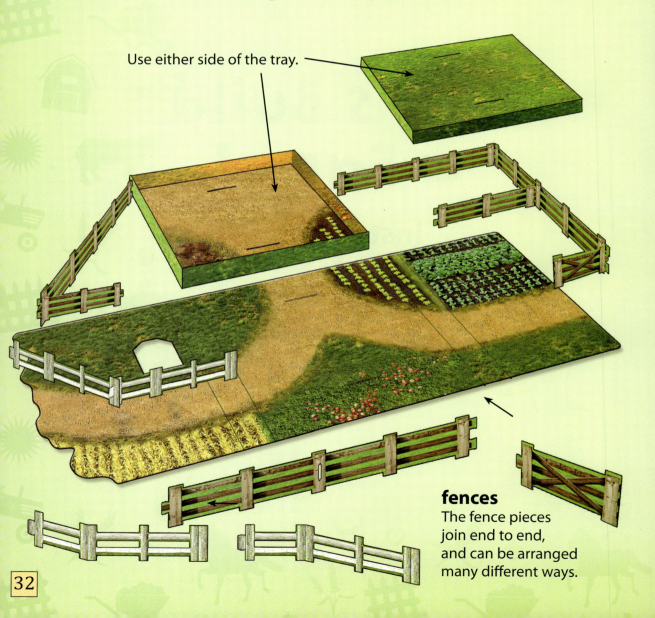

fences
The fence pieces join end to end, and can be arranged many different ways.

barn

1. Press out the wall pieces and arrange them as shown. Using the numbers on the pictures here, match the slots and assemble.

2. Join the two roof pieces together by sliding the tabs into the matching slots as shown.

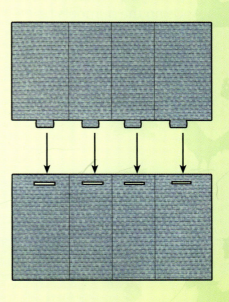

3. Bend the roof along the fold lines as shown, then place on top of the walls.

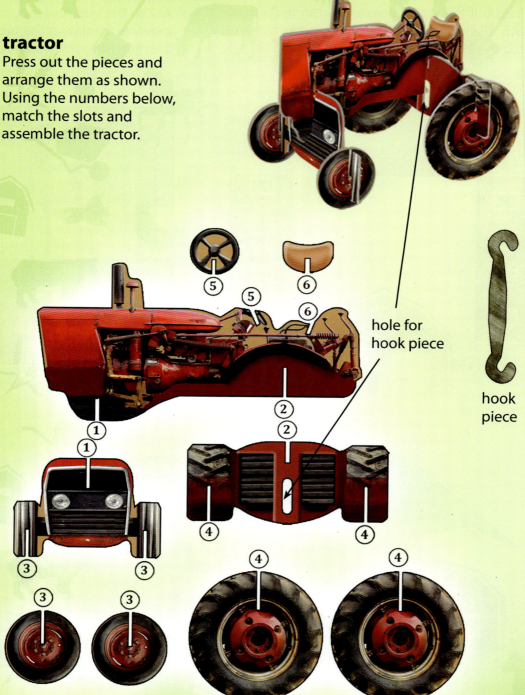

tractor

Press out the pieces and arrange them as shown. Using the numbers below, match the slots and assemble the tractor.

hole for hook piece

hook piece

34

wagon

1. Orient the wagon piece so the wheels are on the left and right sides.

2. Fold the wheels on the left side to the right, along the inner fold line.

3. Now fold the same wheels to the left, along the outer fold line.

3. Do the same folding on the other side, then stand up the wagon and push the tabs through the slots.

hole for hook piece

The wagon can connect to the tractor with the hook piece.

chicken coop

Fold the panels into a "box shape" and push the tabs into the matching numbered slots.

Fold the chickens and egg basket up so they stand.

pig trough

Fold up the sides and tuck the end tabs into the slots as shown.

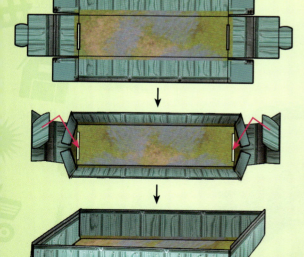

Attach the stands to the pig pieces as shown.

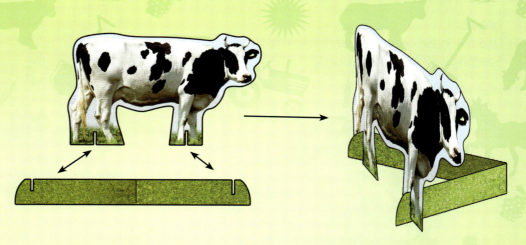

For each of the pieces on this page, there is a base with one center fold line. Fold the base and then match up the slots as shown with the piece above.

trees

Use the base pieces to stand up the trees.
See page 37 for instructions.

The top of the ladder piece can be tucked into a slot in the middle of either apple tree piece.

One of the apple tree pieces has an extended side slot for the basket of apples.

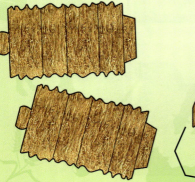

hay bales

Fold each bale along the fold lines and slide the tab into the slot.

Once all your pieces are assembled, arrange your farm any way you like. Add the plastic animals to complete your scene. Most farms have a name. What would you like to name yours?

Silver Dolphin Books

An imprint of Printers Row Publishing Group

10350 Barnes Canyon Road, Suite 100, San Diego, CA 92121

www.silverdolphinbooks.com

Printers Row Publishing Group is a division of Readerlink Distribution Services, LLC.
The Silver Dolphin Books name and logo are trademarks of Readerlink Distribution Services, LLC.

All notations of errors or omissions should be addressed to Silver Dolphin Books, Editorial Department, at the above address. All other correspondence (author inquiries, permissions) concerning the content of this book should be addressed to
Studio Fun International, Inc., 44 S. Broadway, White Plains, NY 10601
www.studiofun.com

ISBN: 978-1-62686-727-7

Manufactured, printed, and assembled in Shenzhen, China
20 19 18 17 16 1 2 3 4 5
HH1/04/16

ILLUSTRATION AND PHOTOGRAPH CREDITS

(t=top, b=bottom, m=middle, l=left, r=right, c=center)

Front Case Cover: ©Flaxphotos/Shutterstock.com; ©Filed IMAGE/Shutterstock.com, ©MaxyM/Shutterstock.com
Front Book Cover: ©meirion matthias/Shutterstock.com; **Back Book Cover:** ©9MongKP/Shutterstock.com
Page 1: ©9MongKP/Shutterstock.com; **Pages 2, 3:** ©Goodluz/Shutterstock.com 2l; ©Orhan Cam/Shutterstock.com 2-3c;
Pages 4, 5: ©BMJ/Shutterstock.com 4l; ©ollirg/Shutterstock.com 4r; MR. SUWIT GAEWSEE-NGAM/Shutterstock.com 4-5c;
©Bochkarev Photography/Shutterstock.com 5br; ©Pressmaster/Shutterstock.com 5tl;
Pages 6, 7: ©Bjorn Heller/Shutterstock.com 6tr; ©sergioboccardo/Shutterstock.com 6bl; ©Chukov/Shutterstock.com 6bc;
©jo Crebbin/Shutterstock.com 7tl; ©TTstudio/Shutterstock.com 7bl; ©Alexander Raths/Shutterstock.com 7br;
Pages 8, 9: ©Le Do/Shutterstock.com 8bl; ©Brian Goodman/Shutterstock.com 8-9c; **Pages 10, 11:** ©Dudarev Mikhail/Shutterstock.com 10-11c;
©WitthayaP/Shutterstock.com 11br; **Pages 12, 13:** ©r.classen/Shutterstock.com 12-13c; ©nulinukas/Shutterstock.com 12tr;
©Andrey Prokhorov/Shutterstock.com13tl; ©panbazil/Shutterstock.com 13tr; **Pages 14, 15:** ©Mats/Shutterstock.com 14tr; ©majeczka/Shutterstock.com 14b; ©Anna
Jurkovska/Shutterstock.com 15t; **Pages 16, 17:** ©Wallenrock/Shutterstock.com 16t; ©Emese/Shutterstock.com 16br;
©l. akhundova/Shutterstock.com 17t; ©Miroslav Hlavko/Shutterstock.com 17br;**Pages 18, 19:** ©tratong/Shutterstock.com 18tl;
©Sergii Figurnyi/Shutterstock.com 18b; ©jadimages/Shutterstock.com 19t; ©Iurii Konoval/Shutterstock.com 19br;
Pages 20, 21: ©Tony Campbell/Shutterstock.com 20tl; ©inobjective/Shutterstock.com 20tc; ©Valentina_S/Shutterstock.com 20br;
©Pack-Shot/Shutterstock.com 20-21tc; ©Serg64/Shutterstock.com 21bl; ©DenisNata/Shutterstock.com 21cr; © PCHT/Shutterstock.com 21br;
Pages 22, 23: ©Lehrer/Shutterstock.com 22c; ©Steve Oehlenschlager/Shutterstock.com 23t; ©Sunny studio-Igor Yaruta/Shutterstock.com & ©lozas/Shutterstock.com
23br; **Pages 24, 25:** ©kaband/Shutterstock.com 24tr; ©Petr Jilek/Shutterstock.com 24b;
©Catalin Petolea/Shutterstock.com 25cl; ©worldswildlifewonders/Shutterstock.com 25r; **Pages 26, 27:** ©Humannet/Shutterstock.com 26tr;
©Smileus/Shutterstock.com 26bl; ©Gordana Sermek/Shutterstock.com 26br; ©hopsalka/Shutterstock.com 27tr;
©Hamiza Bakirci/Shutterstock.com 27c; ©Mazzzur/Shutterstock.com 27br; **Pages 28, 29:** ©Jack schiffer/Shutterstock.com 28l;
©Donya Nedomam/Shutterstock.com 28br; ©Baloncici/Shutterstock.com 29t; ©Goodluz/Shutterstock.com 29br.

Play Scene and Model Imagery: ©Aksenova Natalya/Shutterstock.com, ©Alexander Raths/Shutterstock.com, ©Andrey Prokhorov/Shutterstock.com,
©DenisNata/Shutterstock.com, ©Eduard Kim/Shutterstock.com, ©goodgold99/Shutterstock.com, ©Helga Chirk/Shutterstock.com, ©inobjective/Shutterstock.com,
©MaxyM/Shutterstock.com, ©meirion matthias/Shutterstock.com, ©Mikael Damkier/Shutterstock.com, ©N.Minton/Shutterstock.com, ©Production Perig/Shutterstock.
com, ©Robynrg/Shutterstock.com, ©Ruud Morijn Photographer/Shutterstock.com, ©STANZI/Shutterstock.com, ©Studio Barcelona/Shutterstock.com,
©Szocs Jozsef/Shutterstock.com, ©Valentina_S/Shutterstock.com